MAD LIBS®

HAUNTED MAD LIBS

By Roger Price and Leonard Stern

Mad
An Imprint of Penguin Random House

MAD LIBS
Penguin Young Readers Group
An Imprint of Penguin Random House LLC

Previously published as *Spooky Silly Mad Libs*

Concept created by Roger Price & Leonard Stern

Published by Mad Libs,
an imprint of Penguin Random House LLC,
345 Hudson Street, New York, New York 10014.
Printed in the USA.

ISBN 9780843149067
20

MAD LIBS
INSTRUCTIONS

MAD LIBS® is a game for people who don't like games!
It can be played by one, two, three, four, or forty.

• RIDICULOUSLY SIMPLE DIRECTIONS

In this tablet you will find stories containing blank spaces where words are
left out. One player, the READER, selects one of these stories. The READER
does not tell anyone what the story is about. Instead, he/she asks the other
players, the WRITERS, to give him/her words. These words are used to fill
in the blank spaces in the story.

• TO PLAY

The READER asks each WRITER in turn to call out a word—an adjective or
a noun or whatever the space calls for—and uses them to fill in the blank
spaces in the story. The result is a MAD LIBS® game.

When the READER then reads the completed MAD LIBS® game to the other
players, they will discover that they have written a story that is fantastic,
screamingly funny, shocking, silly, crazy, or just plain dumb—depending
upon which words each WRITER called out.

• EXAMPLE (*Before* and *After*)

"_____!" he said _____
        EXCLAMATION   ADVERB

as he jumped into his convertible _____ and
                                              NOUN

drove off with his _____ wife.
                          ADJECTIVE

"_____*Ouch!*_____!" he said _____*Stupidly*_____
        EXCLAMATION   ADVERB

as he jumped into his convertible _____*cat*_____ and
                                              NOUN

drove off with his _____*brave*_____ wife.
                          ADJECTIVE

MAD LIBS®
QUICK REVIEW

In case you have forgotten what adjectives, adverbs, nouns, and verbs are, here is a quick review:

An ADJECTIVE describes something or somebody. *Lumpy, soft, ugly, messy,* and *short* are adjectives.

An ADVERB tells how something is done. It modifies a verb and usually ends in "ly." *Modestly, stupidly, greedily,* and *carefully* are adverbs.

A NOUN is the name of a person, place or thing. *Sidewalk, umbrella, bridle, bathtub,* and *nose* are nouns.

A VERB is an action word. *Run, pitch, jump,* and *swim* are verbs. Put the verbs in past tense if the directions say PAST TENSE. *Ran, pitched, jumped,* and *swam* are verbs in the past tense.

When we ask for a PLACE, we mean any sort of place: a country or city *(Spain, Cleveland)* or a room *(bathroom, kitchen.)*

An EXCLAMATION or SILLY WORD is any sort of funny sound, gasp, grunt, or outcry, like *Wow!, Ouch!, Whomp!, Ick!,* and *Gadzooks!*

When we ask for specific words, like a NUMBER, a COLOR, an ANIMAL, or a PART OF THE BODY, we mean a word that is one of those things, like *seven, blue, horse,* or *head.*

When we ask for a PLURAL, it means more than one. For example, *cat* pluralized is *cats.*

MAD LIBS® is fun to play with friends, but you can also play it by yourself! To begin with, DO NOT look at the story on the page below. Fill in the blanks on this page with the words called for. Then, using the words you have selected, fill in the blank spaces in the story.

Now you've created your own hilarious MAD LIBS® game!

THE BARBARIAN, PART ONE

PLURAL NOUN _____

SILLY NAME _____

LAST NAME OF MALE IN ROOM _____

ADJECTIVE _____

PLURAL NOUN _____

VERB ENDING IN "ING" _____

ADJECTIVE _____

PERSON IN ROOM (FEMALE) _____

NOUN _____

CELEBRITY (MALE) _____

ANIMAL _____

NOUN _____

ADJECTIVE _____

ANOTHER FEMALE IN ROOM _____

CITY _____

PART OF THE BODY _____

PART OF THE BODY (PLURAL) _____

MAD LIBS®
THE BARBARIAN, PART ONE

Fantasies are almost as popular with teenage American _____
PLURAL NOUN

as horror movies. My favorite was "_____ the Barbarian,"
SILLY NAME

starring Arnold _____ . Arnold is a huge
LAST NAME OF MALE IN ROOM

_____ -looking man who has spent most of his life lifting
ADJECTIVE

_____ and _____ in gymnasiums.
PLURAL NOUN   VERB ENDING IN "ING"

In this movie, Arnold is a/an _____ warrior whose
ADJECTIVE

girlfriend, _____ , has been kidnapped by an evil
PERSON IN ROOM (FEMALE)

_____ , played by _____ . It happens like this:
NOUN   CELEBRITY (MALE)

Arnold is riding over a mountain on his loyal _____ , wearing
ANIMAL

a steel _____ on his head. Suddenly, he meets a beautiful girl
NOUN

wearing a/an _____ gown. Her name is _____ ,
ADJECTIVE   ANOTHER FEMALE IN ROOM

and she is the Queen of _____ . Arnold falls _____
CITY   PART OF THE BODY

over _____ in love with her.
PART OF THE BODY (PLURAL)

MAD LIBS® is fun to play with friends, but you can also play it by yourself! To begin with, DO NOT look at the story on the page below. Fill in the blanks on this page with the words called for. Then, using the words you have selected, fill in the blank spaces in the story.

Now you've created your own hilarious MAD LIBS® game!

THE BARBARIAN, PART TWO

MALE CELEBRITY FROM PART ONE _____

SILLY NAME _____

SILLY WORD _____

SAME CITY AS PART ONE _____

ANOTHER SILLY WORD _____

ADJECTIVE _____

PLURAL NOUN _____

VERB _____

VERB ENDING IN "ING" _____

ADJECTIVE _____

PLURAL NOUN _____

ADJECTIVE _____

PLURAL NOUN _____

NOUN _____

PLURAL NOUN _____

NOUN _____

But _____ kidnaps her and takes her to

SAME MALE CELEBRITY FROM PART ONE

_____'s castle on the river _____. Arnold vows

SILLY NAME   SILLY WORD

to rescue the queen before the villain destroys _____.

SAME CITY AS PART ONE

He discovers that the villain calls himself " _____ the

ANOTHER SILLY WORD

_____ " and rules a bunch of religious _____

ADJECTIVE   PLURAL NOUN

who _____ bathrobes. Whenever they see the villain, they

VERB

begin bowing and _____ and chanting "Ooga-

VERB ENDING IN "ING"

Ooga-Ooga." The villain sends his _____ bodyguards out

ADJECTIVE

to get Arnold. They throw their _____ at him, but he

PLURAL NOUN

ducks. They swing their _____ battle-axes, but he sidesteps

ADJECTIVE

them. They use their bows to shoot poison _____ at him,

PLURAL NOUN

but he hides behind a/an _____, then he runs out and ties all

NOUN

the _____ of their bathrobes together and rescues the

PLURAL NOUN

_____. Everything ends _____ for the good guys.

NOUN   ADVERB

MAD LIBS® is fun to play with friends, but you can also play it by yourself! To begin with, DO NOT look at the story on the page below. Fill in the blanks on this page with the words called for. Then, using the words you have selected, fill in the blank spaces in the story.

Now you've created your own hilarious MAD LIBS® game!

SCENE FROM A HORROR PICTURE

PERSON IN ROOM (MALE)_____

ADJECTIVE_____

HOLIDAY_____

NOUN _____

PLURAL NOUN _____

NOUN _____

PART OF THE BODY _____

SCHOOL SUBJECT _____

SCHOOL _____

NOUN _____

ADJECTIVE_____

NOUN _____

MAD LIBS®
SCENE FROM A
HORROR PICTURE

To be read aloud by a male and a female:

GIRL: Oh, _____ , why did we have to come to this
            PERSON IN ROOM (MALE)

      _____ old castle?
        ADJECTIVE

BOY: All the hotels were closed because of _____ .
                                        HOLIDAY

GIRL: Just look at that sign. It says "The Howard Dracula Holiday

      _____ ."
        NOUN

BOY: Here comes the bellboy for our _____ .
                                   PLURAL NOUN

GIRL: My, he is all bent over and has a big _____ riding on
                                       NOUN

      his _____ .
           PART OF THE BODY

BOY: I think he is my old _____ teacher from
                         SCHOOL SUBJECT

      _____ .
        SCHOOL

GIRL: Watch out! He's throwing a/an _____ over your head.
                                   NOUN

BOY: No, no. He's just being _____ .
                        ADJECTIVE

GIRL: Now he's dragging you toward a bottomless _____ !
                                              NOUN

BOY: I was right. It is my old teacher. Help!

MAD LIBS® is fun to play with friends, but you can also play it by yourself! To begin with, DO NOT look at the story on the page below. Fill in the blanks on this page with the words called for. Then, using the words you have selected, fill in the blank spaces in the story.

Now you've created your own hilarious MAD LIBS® game!

HOT HEAD

ADJECTIVE _____

NUMBER_____

FIRST NAME (FEMALE)_____

LAST NAME_____

NOUN _____

FIRST NAME (MALE)_____

SAME LAST NAME _____

ADJECTIVE _____

ADJECTIVE _____

PLURAL NOUN_____

PLURAL NOUN_____

NOUN _____

ANIMAL_____

VERB ENDING IN "ING" _____

CITY_____

CELEBRITY_____

PROFESSION_____

MAD LIBS®
HOT HEAD

This is a really _____ horror film because the heroine is a little
ADJECTIVE

_____ -year-old girl played by _____ _____
NUMBER FIRST NAME (FEMALE) LAST NAME

who is the granddaughter of the famous old-time _____ ,
NOUN

_____ _____ . In this picture, she can start
FIRST NAME (MALE) SAME LAST NAME

fires by sending _____ vibrations out of the _____
ADJECTIVE ADJECTIVE

part of her little brain. She sets houses on fire and automobiles and

_____ and burns down several _____ . Then
PLURAL NOUN PLURAL NOUN

men from the Defense Department come and want to use her as a

secret military _____ . They tell her if she helps them they
NOUN

will give her a new _____ to play with. But she is too busy
ANIMAL

_____ down _____ and French frying
VERB ENDING IN "ING" CITY

_____ . It all comes to an end when she gives up starting
CELEBRITY

fires and decides to grow up and become a/an _____ .
PROFESSION

MAD LIBS® is fun to play with friends, but you can also play it by yourself! To begin with, DO NOT look at the story on the page below. Fill in the blanks on this page with the words called for. Then, using the words you have selected, fill in the blank spaces in the story.

Now you've created your own hilarious MAD LIBS® game!

THE BLOB

SOMETHING ALIVE (PLURAL) _____

COLOR _____

TYPE OF ICKY FOOD _____

ADJECTIVE _____

CITY _____

CELEBRITY (MALE) _____

TYPE OF LIQUID _____

TYPE OF FOOD (PLURAL) _____

VERB ENDING IN "ING" _____

NOUN _____

ANIMAL _____

ADVERB _____

EXCLAMATION _____

PART OF THE BODY _____

PLURAL NOUN _____

CELEBRITY (FEMALE) _____

PLURAL NOUN _____

MAD LIBS®
THE BLOB

"The Blob" is one of those movies Hollywood _____
                                          SOMETHING ALIVE (PLURAL)

keep remaking every few years. The main character is a huge,

_____ lump of pulsating _____ that wants to become
   COLOR   TYPE OF ICKY FOOD

the first _____ mayor of the city of _____. It was created
          ADJECTIVE   CITY

by a scientist, played by _____. The scientist accidentally
                          CELEBRITY (MALE)

dropped some _____ into a dishful of _____.
             TYPE OF LIQUID   TYPE OF FOOD (PLURAL)

The food immediately started _____ and eventually
                             VERB ENDING IN "ING"

grew to be the size of a/an _____. The Blob eats up the scientist
                            NOUN

and his favorite _____ and begins to roll _____ down
                 ANIMAL   ADVERB

the street. When people see it they say, "_____!" But the
                                          EXCLAMATION

Blob just opens its _____ and swallows them, along with
                   PART OF THE BODY

any_____ that are in the neighborhood. Finally, it gets to the
   PLURAL NOUN

power company where the heroine, played by _____,
                                           CELEBRITY (FEMALE)

manages to kill it with 100,000 _____.
                                PLURAL NOUN

MAD LIBS® is fun to play with friends, but you can also play it by yourself! To begin with, DO NOT look at the story on the page below. Fill in the blanks on this page with the words called for. Then, using the words you have selected, fill in the blank spaces in the story.

Now you've created your own hilarious MAD LIBS® game!

THE GLEAMING

LAST NAME OF MALE IN ROOM_____

NOUN _____

NOUN _____

ADJECTIVE_____

BUILDING_____

RELATIVE_____

ADVERB_____

NUMBER _____

ADJECTIVE_____

ADJECTIVE_____

NOUN _____

ADJECTIVE_____

PROFESSION _____

PART OF THE BODY _____

ADVERB_____

SAME RELATIVE_____

VERB ENDING IN "ING" _____

VERB ENDING IN "ING" _____

VERB (PAST TENSE)_____

ANIMAL _____

MAD LIBS®
THE GLEAMING

One of _____ 's first big roles was playing the
　　　　　　LAST NAME OF MALE IN ROOM

part of the _____ in the horror classic called "The Gleaming
　　　　　　　　NOUN

_____." This _____ movie tells the story of a writer
　NOUN　　　　　　　ADJECTIVE

who needs a quiet place to work, so he rents a/an _____
　　　　　　　　　　　　　　　　　　　　　　　　　　　BUILDING

in Colorado in the middle of winter. He takes his wife and small

_____ with him. Then it snows _____ for _____ days,
　RELATIVE　　　　　　　　　　　　ADVERB　　　　　NUMBER

and the couple discovers the _____ place is haunted by the
　　　　　　　　　　　　　　　　ADJECTIVE

ghost of a/an _____ _____. Well, this _____
　　　　　　　　ADJECTIVE　　　NOUN　　　　　　　　　　ADJECTIVE

ghost is the evil spirit of a former _____ in the Revolutionary
　　　　　　　　　　　　　　　　　　　PROFESSION

Army. It takes possession of his _____ and forces him to
　　　　　　　　　　　　　　　　PART OF THE BODY

act _____ towards his own _____. At this point, there
　　ADVERB　　　　　　　　　　　　SAME RELATIVE

is a lot of _____ and _____, but before he
　　　　　　VERB ENDING IN "ING"　　VERB ENDING IN "ING"

can harm anyone he is _____ by a stray _____.
　　　　　　　　　　　　VERB (PAST TENSE)　　　　　　　ANIMAL

MAD LIBS® is fun to play with friends, but you can also play it by yourself! To begin with, DO NOT look at the story on the page below. Fill in the blanks on this page with the words called for. Then, using the words you have selected, fill in the blank spaces in the story.

Now you've created your own hilarious MAD LIBS® game!

MONSTER MOVIE QUIZ #1

NOUN _____

NOUN _____

CELEBRITY _____

ADJECTIVE_____

CELEBRITY (MALE)_____

BUILDING_____

ANIMAL (PLURAL) _____

CELEBRITY (MALE)_____

NOUN _____

ACTOR (FEMALE) _____

TYPE OF CONTAINER _____

CELEBRITY _____

MAD LIBS®
MONSTER MOVIE QUIZ #1

QUESTION: In the movie, "The _____ of Frankenstein,"
NOUN

who played the part of the local _____?
NOUN

ANSWER: _____.
CELEBRITY

QUESTION: In "The _____ Vampire," what happened to
ADJECTIVE

_____?
CELEBRITY (MALE)

ANSWER: He was thrown off the top of the _____
BUILDING

and eaten by hungry _____.
ANIMAL (PLURAL)

QUESTION: What was _____'s most popular picture?
CELEBRITY (MALE)

ANSWER: It was called "The _____ of Blood." He
NOUN

played a vampire who bit _____ in the
CELEBRITY (FEMALE)

neck and then went to sleep in a/an _____
TYPE OF CONTAINER

buried in the _____ of an old castle.
ROOM

MAD LIBS® is fun to play with friends, but you can also play it by yourself! To begin with, DO NOT look at the story on the page below. Fill in the blanks on this page with the words called for. Then, using the words you have selected, fill in the blank spaces in the story.

Now you've created your own hilarious MAD LIBS® game!

MONSTER MOVIE QUIZ #2

CELEBRITY _____

ADJECTIVE _____

PLURAL NOUN _____

PLURAL NOUN _____

PLURAL NOUN _____

ADJECTIVE _____

ANOTHER CELEBRITY _____

ADJECTIVE _____

NOUN _____

MAD☺LIBS®

MONSTER MOVIE QUIZ #2

QUESTION: Did _____ ever appear in a/an
         CELEBRITY

_____ movie?
ADJECTIVE

ANSWER: Yes. It was called "Arsenic and Old _____."
               PLURAL NOUN

It was about two elderly _____ who kept
         PLURAL NOUN

killing _____ and burying them in the
    PLURAL NOUN

cellar. It was actually more of a comedy than a/an

_____ film.
ADJECTIVE

QUESTION: What was _____'s favorite role?
       ANOTHER CELEBRITY

ANSWER: The part of the _____ mummy in the famous
        ADJECTIVE

movie called "_____."
      NOUN

MAD LIBS® is fun to play with friends, but you can also play it by yourself! To begin with, DO NOT look at the story on the page below. Fill in the blanks on this page with the words called for. Then, using the words you have selected, fill in the blank spaces in the story.

Now you've created your own hilarious MAD LIBS® game!

LETTER TO
A FAMOUS SCARY GUY

LAST NAME _____

NOUN _____

ADJECTIVE_____

ADJECTIVE_____

ANIMAL (PLURAL) _____

PLACE _____

ANOTHER ANIMAL_____

ADJECTIVE_____

SILLY WORD_____

PLURAL NOUN _____

ARTICLE OF CLOTHING_____

PERSON IN ROOM _____

NUMBER _____

ADJECTIVE_____

VERB ENDING IN "ING"_____

ADJECTIVE_____

PERSON IN ROOM (MALE)_____

MAD LIBS®
LETTER TO
A FAMOUS SCARY GUY

Dear Mr. _____:
        LAST NAME

You are my favorite Hollywood _____ because you have done
                                  NOUN

so many _____ horror films. I loved you in "The _____
          ADJECTIVE   ADJECTIVE

Museum" and "The _____ from _____ " and "The Night
                  ANIMAL (PLURAL)   PLACE

the Vampires Met the _____ Man." My particular favorite
                      ANOTHER ANIMAL

was the _____ role you played in "Doctor _____ and
          ADJECTIVE   SILLY WORD

the Yucky, Slimy, Really Horrible _____." You wore a long
                                   PLURAL NOUN

white _____ and had a beard that made you look
        ARTICLE OF CLOTHING

like _____ . I saw that _____ times. You are
        PERSON IN ROOM   NUMBER

a/an _____ good actor and should get the Academy Award for
       ADJECTIVE

_____ . I think you are almost as scary as my other
VERB ENDING IN "ING"

favorite _____ actor, _____ Mouse.
          ADJECTIVE   PERSON IN ROOM (MALE)

From HAUNTED MAD LIBS® • Copyright © 2002, 1989 by Penguin Random House LLC.

MAD LIBS® is fun to play with friends, but you can also play it by yourself! To begin with, DO NOT look at the story on the page below. Fill in the blanks on this page with the words called for. Then, using the words you have selected, fill in the blank spaces in the story.

Now you've created your own hilarious MAD LIBS® game!

THE SPOOKY OPERA, PART ONE

NOUN _____

NOUN _____

NUMBER _____

CELEBRITY (MALE) _____

ADJECTIVE _____

ADJECTIVE _____

NOUN _____

TYPE OF MACHINE _____

PERSON IN ROOM _____

ARTICLE OF CLOTHING _____

TYPE OF FOOD _____

PERSON IN ROOM (FEMALE) _____

ADJECTIVE _____

TYPE OF FOOD (PLURAL) _____

TYPE OF LIQUID _____

MAD LIBS®
THE SPOOKY OPERA, PART ONE

"The _____ of the Opera" was a silent _____ made
              NOUN   NOUN

_____ years ago, and it starred _____ as a/an
   NUMBER   CELEBRITY (MALE)

_____ monster who had formerly been a/an _____
  ADJECTIVE   ADJECTIVE

singing _____ at the opera. But he got his face caught in
              NOUN

a/an _____ and when he recovered, he looked like
        TYPE OF MACHINE

_____. So he hid in the tunnels beneath the opera house
  PERSON IN ROOM

and wore a long _____ and lived on dried beans and
                    ARTICLE OF CLOTHING

_____. One day he saw _____ and fell in
  TYPE OF FOOD   PERSON IN ROOM (FEMALE)

love with her. So he kidnapped her and took her to his _____
                                                            ADJECTIVE

underground home. The monster was nice to the girl and brought

her delicious _____ and _____.
                 TYPE OF FOOD (PLURAL)   TYPE OF LIQUID

MAD LIBS® is fun to play with friends, but you can also play it by yourself! To begin with, DO NOT look at the story on the page below. Fill in the blanks on this page with the words called for. Then, using the words you have selected, fill in the blank spaces in the story.

Now you've created your own hilarious MAD LIBS® game!

THE SPOOKY OPERA, PART TWO

NOUN _____

NOUN _____

ADJECTIVE _____

NOUN _____

PART OF THE BODY _____

PERSON IN ROOM (MALE)_____

VERB ENDING IN "ING" _____

ADVERB_____

ADJECTIVE_____

NOUN _____

EXCLAMATION_____

VERB _____

NOUN _____

CELEBRITY (MALE) _____

ADVERB_____

NUMBER _____

MAD LIBS®
THE SPOOKY OPERA, PART TWO

Now that the monster had kidnapped the _____ he loved,
                                          NOUN

he had to wear a/an _____ to cover his face because he was
                        NOUN

so _____. Naturally, the girl thought he was nothing but a/an
    ADJECTIVE

_____ who was probably a little touched in the _____.
   NOUN   PART OF THE BODY

Meanwhile, her fiancé, played by _____ , suspected
                                   PERSON IN ROOM (MALE)

what had happened and began _____ the tunnels for
                              VERB ENDING IN "ING"

her. But the monster had _____ prepared a/an _____
                            ADVERB   ADJECTIVE

trap, so when the fiancé went into the room, a huge _____
                                                       NOUN

slammed down behind him.

"_____!" the monster said to the girl. "Now you will have
    EXCLAMATION

to marry me or I will _____ your fiancé."
                         VERB

"No, no!" the girl cried. "That would be a/an _____ worse
                                                 NOUN

than death!"

But the monster took off his mask and the girl saw that he looked

just like _____ , so she married him. And they lived
            CELEBRITY (MALE)

_____ for _____ years.
   ADVERB   NUMBER

MAD LIBS® is fun to play with friends, but you can also play it by yourself! To begin with, DO NOT look at the story on the page below. Fill in the blanks on this page with the words called for. Then, using the words you have selected, fill in the blank spaces in the story.

Now you've created your own hilarious MAD LIBS® game!

PUPPY LOVE

SILLY NAME _____

ADJECTIVE _____

ADJECTIVE _____

BUILDING _____

ADJECTIVE _____

ADJECTIVE _____

NOUN _____

SAME SILLY NAME _____

PLURAL NOUN _____

PLURAL NOUN _____

ADJECTIVE _____

TYPE OF DISEASE _____

NOUN _____

NOUN _____

PLURAL NOUN _____

TYPE OF FOOD (PLURAL) _____

ADJECTIVE _____

TYPE OF MACHINE _____

ARTICLE OF CLOTHING (PLURAL) _____

SAME SILLY NAME _____

VERB ENDING IN "ING" _____

MAD LIBS®
PUPPY LOVE

_____ was a huge, _____ St. Bernard dog who belonged

SILLY NAME   ADJECTIVE

to a/an _____ man who worked in a/an _____.

        ADJECTIVE   BUILDING

The man had a/an _____ loving wife and two _____

                ADJECTIVE   ADJECTIVE

children. The oldest was a boy, the other was a/an _____.

                                                  NOUN

_____ loved them all and would fetch the man's

SAME SILLY NAME

_____ and guard the house against _____ and

PLURAL NOUN   PLURAL NOUN

_____ burglars. Then, one day, he caught _____

ADJECTIVE   TYPE OF DISEASE

and changed from a sweet, loving _____ into a ferocious,

                                NOUN

evil _____. He tried to bite the _____ and stole

     NOUN   PLURAL NOUN

_____ from the kitchen. He seemed to be inhabited

TYPE OF FOOD (PLURAL)

by a/an _____ spirit. He trapped the mother in the family

        ADJECTIVE

_____ and scared the _____ off the

TYPE OF MACHINE   ARTICLE OF CLOTHING (PLURAL)

father. But the family managed to escape. A lady dog came by and

_____ began _____ and winking,

SAME SILLY NAME   VERB ENDING IN "ING"

and he decided to leave the family alone.

MAD LIBS® is fun to play with friends, but you can also play it by yourself! To begin with, DO NOT look at the story on the page below. Fill in the blanks on this page with the words called for. Then, using the words you have selected, fill in the blank spaces in the story.

Now you've created your own hilarious MAD LIBS® game!

THE KING OF CREEPY

FIRST NAME (MALE) _____

ADJECTIVE _____

ADJECTIVE _____

TYPE OF CEREAL _____

ANIMAL _____

PLURAL NOUN _____

PLACE _____

VERB ENDING IN "ING" _____

LAST NAME _____

ANOTHER LAST NAME _____

ADJECTIVE _____

NUMBER _____

PLURAL NOUN _____

ADJECTIVE _____

ADJECTIVE _____

NOUN _____

TYPE OF LIQUID _____

ADVERB _____

MAD LIBS®
THE KING OF CREEPY

_____ King has written some really _____,
   FIRST NAME (MALE)   ADJECTIVE

spooky books which have been made into super- _____
                                                      ADJECTIVE

movies. For instance, there was "Children of the _____"
                                               TYPE OF CEREAL

and "Cujo the _____." And then there was another one
                       ANIMAL

about _____, which was called "Pet _____." A very
            PLURAL NOUN   PLACE

successful movie was "The _____," which starred Jack
                              VERB ENDING IN "ING"

_____ and Shelly _____. It was Jack's first
   LAST NAME   ANOTHER LAST NAME

big movie and since then he has become a/an _____ star
                                          ADJECTIVE

and has been nominated for _____ Academy _____.
                             NUMBER   PLURAL NOUN

There are other very _____ scary films that Mr. King did not
                       ADJECTIVE

write. For instance, the _____ classic called "The Chain Saw
                        ADJECTIVE

_____," which can really curdle a person's _____.
   NOUN   TYPE OF LIQUID

If you see any of these movies, chances are you won't sleep very

_____ that night.
   ADVERB

MAD LIBS® is fun to play with friends, but you can also play it by yourself! To begin with, DO NOT look at the story on the page below. Fill in the blanks on this page with the words called for. Then, using the words you have selected, fill in the blank spaces in the story.

Now you've created your own hilarious MAD LIBS® game!

PROM NIGHT, PART ONE

PERSON IN ROOM (FEMALE)_____

SOMETHING ALIVE _____

ADJECTIVE_____

SCHOOL _____

PLURAL NOUN _____

VERB ENDING IN "ING" _____

ADVERB_____

PLURAL NOUN _____

ADJECTIVE_____

SILLY WORD_____

NOUN _____

ADJECTIVE_____

ARTICLE OF CLOTHING (PLURAL)_____

ADJECTIVE_____

ADVERB_____

MAD LIBS®
PROM NIGHT, PART ONE

One of the first and finest major horror films of all time was called

" _____ ," about a teenage _____
   PERSON IN ROOM (FEMALE)   SOMETHING ALIVE

who was _____ . She went to _____ and she
         ADJECTIVE   SCHOOL

got good grades in _____ and _____ , but
                    PLURAL NOUN   VERB ENDING IN "ING"

she was always behaving _____ and did not like her
                          ADVERB

fellow _____ . This was because they did not like her.
        PLURAL NOUN

They all thought she was _____ and a/an _____ .
                          ADJECTIVE   SILLY WORD

So at the end of her senior _____ , this girl was not invited to
                             NOUN

the _____ prom. All of the other students had dates and new
     ADJECTIVE

_____ to wear. But they treated their classmate
ARTICLE OF CLOTHING (PLURAL)

as if she were really _____ . And she behaved so _____ ,
                       ADJECTIVE   ADVERB

it was horrifying.

MAD LIBS® is fun to play with friends, but you can also play it by yourself! To begin with, DO NOT look at the story on the page below. Fill in the blanks on this page with the words called for. Then, using the words you have selected, fill in the blank spaces in the story.

Now you've created your own hilarious MAD LIBS® game!

PROM NIGHT, PART TWO

SAME FEMALE NAME FROM PART ONE _____

PLURAL NOUN _____

SOCIAL OCCASION _____

ADJECTIVE_____

PART OF THE BODY _____

PLURAL NOUN _____

VERB ENDING IN "ING" _____

ROOM _____

PART OF THE BODY (PLURAL) _____

PLURAL NOUN _____

PLURAL NOUN _____

COLOR_____

TYPE OF LIQUID _____

NOUN _____

VERB ENDING IN "ING" _____

VERB ENDING IN "ING" _____

NOUN _____

VERB ENDING IN "ING" _____

EXCLAMATION_____

SAME FEMALE IN NAME _____

MAD LIBS®
PROM NIGHT, PART TWO

_____ was so mad at all of the other
SAME FEMALE NAME FROM PART ONE

_____ at her school that she decided to ruin their
PLURAL NOUN

_____ . You see, she had _____ magical powers
SOCIAL OCCASION   ADJECTIVE

and if she concentrated on her _____ , she could start
PART OF THE BODY

fires or make _____ start _____ . So she
PLURAL NOUN   VERB ENDING IN "ING"

went to the place where the dance was being held and got into the

_____ and her _____ blazed out magical
ROOM   PART OF THE BODY (PLURAL)

energy and all of the girl's _____ burst into _____ .
PLURAL NOUN   PLURAL NOUN

Then _____ _____ began dripping from
COLOR   TYPE OF LIQUID

the _____ all over everyone. At this point, everyone began
NOUN

_____ and _____ and trying to get out,
VERB ENDING IN "ING"   VERB ENDING IN "ING"

but there was only one little _____ . The students were
NOUN

_____ on each other and screaming, "_____!"
VERB ENDING IN "ING"   EXCLAMATION

It really taught those students a lesson. The lesson was, "Don't forget

to invite _____ ."
SAME FEMALE NAME

MAD LIBS® is fun to play with friends, but you can also play it by yourself! To begin with, DO NOT look at the story on the page below. Fill in the blanks on this page with the words called for. Then, using the words you have selected, fill in the blank spaces in the story.

Now you've created your own hilarious MAD LIBS® game!

BUNDLE OF BAD

ADJECTIVE_____

PART OF THE BODY _____

ADJECTIVE_____

TYPE OF FOOD _____

NOUN _____

ADJECTIVE_____

OCCUPATION _____

RELATIVE _____

SAME OCCUPATION_____

PLACE _____

EXCLAMATION_____

NOUN _____

PART OF THE BODY _____

TYPE OF LIQUID _____

VERB _____

VERB ENDING IN "ING" _____

PLURAL NOUN _____

PLURAL NOUN _____

VERB ENDING IN "ING" _____

MAD☺LIBS®

BUNDLE OF BAD

Well, here we have a horror movie about a poor woman who has this

_____ baby who is starting to grow horns on its
ADJECTIVE

_____. It also has a/an _____ disposition and throws
PART OF THE BODY   ADJECTIVE

its _____ on the floor and bangs its _____
TYPE OF FOOD   NOUN

against the side of its crib. Of course, we all know that the baby is

_____ because a/an _____ is its _____.
ADJECTIVE   OCCUPATION   RELATIVE

Now the movie really gets scary as they call up the _____
                                                          SAME OCCUPATION

from the pits of _____. It looks at the baby and says,
                        PLACE

"_____! The little _____ is a chip off the
    EXCLAMATION   NOUN

old _____." And he insists that the mother drink a glass of
      PART OF THE BODY

_____. Well, then the house begins to _____
TYPE OF LIQUID   VERB

and the walls start _____. All of the teenage
                            VERB ENDING IN "ING"

_____ in the audience scream and hide their _____.
PLURAL NOUN   PLURAL NOUN

This movie was really a very _____ experience.
                                    VERB ENDING IN "ING"

MAD LIBS® is fun to play with friends, but you can also play it by yourself! To begin with, DO NOT look at the story on the page below. Fill in the blanks on this page with the words called for. Then, using the words you have selected, fill in the blank spaces in the story.

Now you've created your own hilarious MAD LIBS® game!

PETS

PLACE _____

ADJECTIVE_____

NOUN _____

ANOTHER PLACE _____

ADJECTIVE_____

SAME PLACE_____

ADJECTIVE_____

SOMETHING UGLY (PLURAL) _____

ADJECTIVE_____

PLURAL NOUN _____

TYPE OF FOOD (PLURAL) _____

PLURAL NOUN _____

PLURAL NOUN _____

VERB ENDING IN "ING" _____

TOWN_____

TYPE OF FOOD _____

ANOTHER TYPE OF FOOD _____

VERB (PAST TENSE)_____

NOUN _____

PART OF THE BODY _____

MAD LIBS®
PETS

A great horror movie called "Pet _____," based on a/an
_____ PLACE
_____ book of the same _____, was about an
ADJECTIVE   NOUN

Indian burial _____. All of the people buried in the
ANOTHER PLACE

_____ Indian _____ came back to life but turned
ADJECTIVE   SAME PLACE

into _____ frightening _____. Well, right
ADJECTIVE   SOMETHING UGLY (PLURAL)

away these _____ monsters began to get hungry, and I bet
ADJECTIVE

you _____ to _____ you can't guess what they
PLURAL NOUN   TYPE OF FOOD (PLURAL)

wanted to eat. Well, okay, so you made a lucky guess. They especially

wanted to eat adorable _____ and cute _____. Let
PLURAL NOUN   PLURAL NOUN

me tell you, it got worse. Those creatures started _____
VERB ENDING IN "ING"

up everything alive in town. People began to get really nervous and

many moved to _____. The others all became _____
TOWN   TYPE OF FOOD

or _____ for the monsters. About this time I left the
ANOTHER TYPE OF FOOD

theater as I was _____ to death and wanted to get home
VERB (PAST TENSE)

to hide under my _____ with a pillow over my _____.
NOUN   PART OF THE BODY

MAD LIBS® is fun to play with friends, but you can also play it by yourself! To begin with, DO NOT look at the story on the page below. Fill in the blanks on this page with the words called for. Then, using the words you have selected, fill in the blank spaces in the story.

Now you've created your own hilarious MAD LIBS® game!

WEIRD PLANTS, PART ONE

ADJECTIVE_____

ADJECTIVE_____

PLURAL NOUN _____

ADJECTIVE_____

NUMBER _____

COLOR_____

ANOTHER COLOR _____

CITY _____

NOUN _____

VERB ENDING IN "ING" _____

VERB _____

ADJECTIVE_____

NOUN _____

SILLY WORD (PLURAL)_____

SAME SILLY WORD (PLURAL) _____

PLURAL NOUN _____

SOMETHING ALIVE (PLURAL) _____

TYPE OF SEASONING _____

HOLIDAY_____

MAD LIBS®
WEIRD PLANTS, PART ONE

The English made some of the earliest and most _____
ADJECTIVE

scary films, such as the _____ film called "The Day of the
ADJECTIVE

_____." This _____ picture was made
PLURAL NOUN   ADJECTIVE

_____ years ago, so it was in _____ and _____.
NUMBER   COLOR   ANOTHER COLOR

It begins when people in the English city of _____ see a strange
CITY

_____ in the sky. It gives out a/an _____ flash of
NOUN   VERB ENDING IN "ING"

light and no one can _____ anymore. A few people are spared
VERB

and they see that hundreds of strange, very big, _____-looking
ADJECTIVE

plants are growing everywhere. They call these strange _____-
NOUN

like things _____. The _____ send out
SILLY WORD (PLURAL)   SAME SILLY WORD (PLURAL)

long vines and capture _____ and even _____.
PLURAL NOUN   SOMETHING ALIVE (PLURAL)

Then they sprinkle them with _____ and have them for
TYPE OF SEASONING

_____ dinner. Well, one man escapes.
HOLIDAY

MAD LIBS® is fun to play with friends, but you can also play it by yourself! To begin with, DO NOT look at the story on the page below. Fill in the blanks on this page with the words called for. Then, using the words you have selected, fill in the blank spaces in the story.

Now you've created your own hilarious MAD LIBS® game!

WEIRD PLANTS, PART TWO

NOUN _____

PLURAL NOUN _____

PLACE _____

ADJECTIVE _____

PLURAL NOUN _____

TYPE OF APPLIANCE _____

CITY _____

ADJECTIVE _____

ADJECTIVE _____

NAME OF AN ORGANIZATION _____

VERB ENDING IN "ING" _____

SAME SILLY WORD FROM PART ONE _____

VERB ENDING IN "ING" _____

PLURAL NOUN _____

PLURAL NOUN _____

ADVERB _____

NUMBER _____

ANOTHER NUMBER _____

MAD LIBS®
WEIRD PLANTS, PART TWO

Do you remember what happened in the last _____? Weird,
NOUN

creepy _____ were growing all over _____ and eating
PLURAL NOUN   PLACE

up the people. But one man escaped and he met a/an _____
ADJECTIVE

girl and they heard other _____ talking on the
PLURAL NOUN

_____. So they searched all over _____ until
TYPE OF APPLIANCE   CITY

they found a bunch of _____ survivors. Then they all
ADJECTIVE

formed a/an _____ group for self defense and called it
ADJECTIVE

_____. By studying and _____
NAME OF AN ORGANIZATION   VERB ENDING IN "ING"

the evil _____, they found they could be
SAME SILLY WORD FROM PART ONE

killed by _____. So they made a weapon out of old
VERB ENDING IN "ING"

_____ and _____ and destroyed the creatures,
PLURAL NOUN   PLURAL NOUN

and humanity lived _____ for the next _____ years.
ADVERB   NUMBER

Maybe it was really _____.
ANOTHER NUMBER

MAD LIBS® is fun to play with friends, but you can also play it by yourself! To begin with, DO NOT look at the story on the page below. Fill in the blanks on this page with the words called for. Then, using the words you have selected, fill in the blank spaces in the story.

Now you've created your own hilarious MAD LIBS® game!

DRAMATIC MOVIE SCENE

PERSON IN ROOM _____

NOUN _____

VERB ENDING IN "ING" _____

NOUN _____

ANIMAL (PLURAL) _____

ADJECTIVE_____

EXCLAMATION_____

PLURAL NOUN _____

ADJECTIVE_____

NOUN _____

SOMETHING ALIVE _____

PART OF THE BODY _____

PLURAL NOUN _____

NAME OF A SONG _____

ADVERB_____

PERSON IN ROOM (MALE)_____

VERB ENDING IN "ING" _____

PLURAL NOUN _____

EXCLAMATION_____

MAD LIBS®
DRAMATIC MOVIE SCENE

Here is a scene from a classic _____ horror movie. The
                                    PERSON IN ROOM

movie is called "The _____ of the _____." It
                        NOUN   VERB ENDING IN "ING"

opens on an old, deserted _____ , and we hear _____
                              NOUN   ANIMAL (PLURAL)

howling. We move in and we see that four people are standing by

a/an _____ grave. One says, "_____!" and the others
        ADJECTIVE   EXCLAMATION

all nod their _____ , and then they shove a/an _____
                PLURAL NOUN   ADJECTIVE

box into the grave. The box is a/an _____ coffin and it is open.
                                        NOUN

Inside is a pale, dead _____ that has a stake through
                          SOMETHING ALIVE

its _____ . Then the people start throwing _____
    PART OF THE BODY   PLURAL NOUN

into the grave and singing _____ . They stop _____
                              NAME OF A SONG   ADVERB

when an enormous bat flies down and says, "I am the spirit of Count

_____ and a member of the _____
  PERSON IN ROOM (MALE)   VERB ENDING IN "ING"

dead. I am going to come back and get all of you _____ ."
                                                    PLURAL NOUN

Then the corpse sits up and shouts, "_____!"
                                        EXCLAMATION

MAD LIBS® is fun to play with friends, but you can also play it by yourself! To begin with, DO NOT look at the story on the page below. Fill in the blanks on this page with the words called for. Then, using the words you have selected, fill in the blank spaces in the story.

Now you've created your own hilarious MAD LIBS® game!

SPOOKY STUFF

ADJECTIVE_____

PLURAL NOUN _____

PLURAL NOUN _____

SILLY WORD_____

TYPE OF LIQUID _____

ADJECTIVE_____

NOUN _____

VERB _____

PLURAL NOUN _____

VERB ENDING IN "ING"_____

NUMBER _____

VERB ENDING IN "ING" _____

PLURAL NOUN _____

NOUN _____

MAD LIBS®

SPOOKY STUFF

American children are fascinated by _____ stuff. Stories

ADJECTIVE

that scare the _____ off them or make their _____

PLURAL NOUN PLURAL NOUN

stand on end. Scientists say this is because being frightened causes

the _____ gland to function and put _____ into

SILLY WORD TYPE OF LIQUID

their blood. And everyone knows this makes a kid feel _____.

ADJECTIVE

When they are scared by a movie or a/an _____, boys laugh

NOUN

and holler and _____. But girls cover their eyes with their

VERB

_____ and keep screaming and _____. Most

PLURAL NOUN VERB ENDING IN "ING"

kids get over this by the time they are _____ years old. Then

NUMBER

they like movies about cars _____ or cops shooting

VERB ENDING IN "ING"

_____ or, if they are girls, they like movies about a boy

PLURAL NOUN

meeting a _____ and falling in love. Of course, that can be

NOUN

scary, too.

Join the millions of Mad Libs fans creating
wacky and wonderful stories on our apps!

Download Mad Libs today!